Inner Journey

Inner Journey

Stepping-Stones into Our Destiny of Love

One Voice with
Kathryn Rawlings and Terry A. Spears

ISBN: 978-0-578-58379-2

For information, contact Kathryn or Terry at
purposerealized@gmail.com

Dedication

All hearts gather together
to seek harmony in life.
This is a salute to those that seek
the truth of who they are.

Contents

Part 1:

Prelude

Preface

Inspiration! How sweet it is! Our spirit, God's vessel of expression, calls us. Listen. Listen. The still, small voice within beckons. Hear me!

Inner Journey: Stepping-Stones into Our Destiny of Love was born from spirit. The whispers, the urgings felt from the still, small voice within grew, shaping, igniting, and bursting forth into resounding, clear messages of love that must be expressed and expressed they were in the written word. Love begets love and cannot be silent.

And we begin.

One Voice

O ne voice of truth rings within our very soul and spirit. We are a society of diversity in expression and uniquely migrate toward our pathways of self-discovery.

Throughout history special beings of light, enlightened ones, have attracted followers to be blessed within their teachings. We follow Godlike expressions of truth through the examples of inspiring messages given. Blossoming like a radiant facet of a diamond, we each express ourselves in a most unique, individual expression of who we are.

Eventually we come to rest, finding our sweet spot hidden within that unravels our hidden secrets, exposing the simplicity of love. This generic, persuasive love runs deeply in and throughout our very existence.

The Oneness of Creator, including many awakened ones, share here as One Voice, a pathway for awakening into compassion and love. This pathway is offered to humanity for anyone on a spiritual quest, for anyone attempting to grow internally and heal into grace and ease of life.

Star Light, Star Bright...
A Brief History

❦

"In the beginning, God created Heaven and earth...And so God created man in His own image, in the image of God He created him; male and female He created them."[ii] The coming changes on earth that will bring humanity into their fullness is quite a masterful event, one that has not taken place before, because it required this intricate evolution to express the fullness of the individual that could not be expressed before, for many reasons.

We, as humans, embody lightness and darkness within, and the darkness of our being was taken into account as the ends of the earth complied with our descent into duality. Mother Earth accommodated all of our polarized human energies in our third dimensional learning processes. The duality energies of third dimensional earth were necessary for our experiences of opposite comparisons, offering multiple choices. Humanity would need to take the densest of energies within and eventually bring these emotions back to love. It was a time that allowed the darkness to prevail, leaving a reality that was devoid of inspiring light. The human race was tampered with, essentially handicapping the race, when humans' intuition was disconnected and monitored and was not allowed to express fully in God's glory.

The resulting denseness of being during these dark times exaggerated the texture of evil and ill-doing upon the land. The darkness within souls was invited forward, and humanity came to a division within expressing as duality. Through the dark ages of existence, the evolution of man came slowly into a time of recovery, so that over time, man pondered the heavens, looking into the vast space above. Twinkling stars gathered attention, and the magic of their fascination was a wellspring of hope into the unknown.

Man studied and mapped the stars in hopes of finding a road map to guide and protect them from the invading evils of the world. The rise and fall of the ruling powers created opportunities that allowed the opening of love. Personal freedom and a personal endeavor to become greater reign above all else. Slowly, as the trickle of light gained in momentum, people began to awaken.

As light infiltrated the soul, new insights came and hope rose up to fulfill the recovery of man's ill-fated demise of existence. Mankind began to receive inspirations in many ways. Prophecies were formed and shared, and the minds of men found some solace in their content. Sometimes the special people who knew the knowledge of light gained in their popularity, and, as history records, many prophets of goodness began to share their inspirations.

Some said the world would be in line for events of cataclysmic proportions, sweeping the earth clean of its evils and starting again to become more holy or righteous within its population. Definitions of righteousness spread rapidly within the confines of man's thinking. Control and war demanded a righteous mind, if it was to be justified as a good and profitable event.

As time passed and the evolution of the human species dwelled in darkness of confusion and wonder, the light continued to filter through, and hope of goodness grew. Now in our current time on earth, we find much similarity to these past events. Do we see the stars as a hopeful light for understanding of the mysteries of life? Do we feel the stirring of our magical, inner sense of the truth of who we are?

"Seek and ye shall find," and the almighty hand of love strikes a chord within the people. Granted, there are stumbling blocks along the way of understanding the bigger picture of life, but we still seek, and we shall find all that we are looking for. The pools of the holy waters of truth and fullness of spirit now rush over our numbed spirits and quench our thirst for the knowledge of life that is revealing itself in these days of resurrection of spirit and rejuvenation of the wounded heart of the past.

In a masterful event, the Creator now steps forward to redeem His own. Reclaiming the ashes of the past and renewing their fiber, He reveals the present moment reality as a new and poignant essence of light and love.

We come now to a time of relinquishing the need of control and bowing to the heart of love. There will be times now when unison and harmony with complete balance and goodwill is what everything is all about.

These messages within this volume are from our Creator, spoken as One Voice, and serve the purpose of awakening our souls into our conscious walk into the sunlight of the soul. The radiance of our being comes alive as we have been masterly designed to become. A time of revealing our true selves and walking this journey of self-revelation into the arms of our Creator is upon us now.

The evolution and destiny of mankind is now moving rapidly into its wholeness of being. Our choice is always present to cooperate with the growth of light within. If we choose, we can walk alive and well into a life of love experienced in our heaven on earth.

Divine Promise

Heaven on earth, living happily in love and peace, life everlasting is understood as our divine promise from God. And of course, many of us do desire and choose this! But how do we achieve this special standing, this consciousness where we can feel this presence of love and walk into heaven?

Searching for love, the universal desire of loving and being loved, of belonging is a driving force in all of humanity. All of our lives are focused at achieving some measure of this vision of the divine promise, but many have become lost in their quest for love, looking for love in all the wrong places [iii] How can this promise be fulfilled? And will it?

A wounded, rejected heart will struggle to heal, to find acceptance, honor, to be admired. Often all hope of finding and feeling relevance, acknowledgment, acceptance, or believing that their lives matter is lost.

In the pain of loss and rejection, a person can become more and more desperate, taking drastic measures to gain some degree of love, and will even settle for notoriety. Any attention is better than no attention. So desperate is the need for love that in their pain, some align with hate-filled idealists, trying to create an exclusivity that helps them stand out as special and therefore desirable. And with the growing pain of rejection, the wounded heart strikes out, even willing to give its own life for validation.

An individual can slip off of their intended path, lose their way, and then apply the ever-quickening energies for less-than-desirable outcomes. Sometimes wayward behaviors are more prevalent. A lost soul, crying for love, can create untold devastation.

Now with heightened frequencies of love bathing the earth and quickening our healing and growth, we are prompted to apply these energies wisely to the opportunities steadily coming forth now. It is time to heal. Where is the love we all long for? That all of life is in quest of? Is God's divine promise of heaven, life everlasting in wholeness and Oneness, obtainable? How?

Herein lie the puzzle pieces of life coming together in a focus of understanding and love. Divine intervention is at work now to help heal wounded hearts and reclaim lost souls. With God, all things are possible. And so it can be with all of us.

Here, with God's blessings and signature of One Voice, He calls you home. May these blessed words of love help heal the wounded hearts, taking the splintered attributes of humanity into their fullest expressions of active virtues.

Dear ones, avail yourselves to these healing words, and let the divine promise of love and everlasting life bless you with relief, peace, and an emerging love within. You can reclaim your preciousness, for in the heart of God, all are precious, and His hand now reaches out to gather you into His embrace. Each of your heartbeats is a sacred event, a miracle in action. You are loved and valued. Feel this lovingness bloom within you, as self-acceptance and understanding of your path, your way home becomes clear and obtainable. Let the holy essence of life enfold you.

The tide has turned, and, as you intend, as you choose love, so can you manifest your desires in alignment with your soul plan of returning home to God.

Open, dear ones, to your destiny of wholeness in love, of belonging in the oneness of God. We are One. And so it is.

The Christis Steps Forward

We, the people, are a people of inspiration and love. We, the people, unite together in our hearts with one true voice of love. We flounder around in our growth processes, but most assuredly we find our core is the most exquisite design of magnificence.

I am the Christ. I have been called many names of identification. As I walked among men, I was called Jesus, the Christ. I am one with the Source of Life, the Almighty One.

I am known as the Father to those that feel My presence as one with the all. I live in harmony with the all. The *isness of being* is the perfect creation of life expressing, one voice united in love, expressed in oneness through the Father, Son, and Spirit, one voice originating in Source, God-Creator of all.

So how am I called? By name of the Intended One, the Intended One of survival of love in all people. I have been assigned the special service of the gathering of souls to harvest the light in all who seek the masterful knowledge of the truth of their being.

This creation is a magnificent creation of love expressed. The creation of life is foretold and is honored. I am as I am and bring to the world the opportunity of love to be expressed in fullness of spirit within all who choose this timing to come home to the radiance of life growing, expanding, and unifying in all hearts.

I am the Christ. I Am that I Am. I assist now in all ways the blessing of all souls to come forward and rise up in self as never before. Consider revisiting the following prayer.

The Lord's Prayer
Our Father, Who art in Heaven,
hallowed be Thy name.
Thy Kingdom come,
Thy will be done on earth,
as it is in Heaven.
Give us this day, our daily bread,
and forgive us our trespasses,
as we forgive those
who trespass against us,
And lead us not into temptation,
but deliver us from evil.
For thine is the Kingdom,
the Power, and the Glory
forever and ever. Amen. iv

This day stands alone in the ability to accept your own wise inner truth and blossom into your fullness of spirit. My heart is your heart, and we are one.

The Christic Continues

~~~

S ince I was a little boy on earth, I felt a strong connection to the ground beneath me. I felt like I was part of it. As I grew, I came to know my life would hold magical abilities to share with others.

As I fulfilled my purpose on earth, I knew the hearts of men were feeling lost and alone. I knew my Father above would use me to help others to reunite with their own connection to the special part of God held within the bosom of all.

It is this knowing of my purpose and connection to humanity and all of life that held my attention, and my heart grew and radiated a deep love for all.

This love, God's love, your love, is alive and well in all living things, for it is the fabric of creation that holds the path and destiny of the evolution of man.

This connection to all is the life-force energy of life in all its glory. This expansion of love grows, ongoing, until one day the world vibrates in unity with all. This process is the process of reclaiming Oneness of Spirit, which allows the structure of life to tell its story, as it weaves its way into a sight to behold.

What Purpose Is There to Life?

All hold the fabric of creative growth and follow the design of evolution into a grander scale of what it is. This is the way of things. All come into their glory of self as they travel the path of their destiny of love expanding.

Life's purpose is life unfolding and changing into a new version of what it is, and is our individual purpose, as we become aware and reach out to share. This is the cycle of life as the breath goes inward and outward, the yin and the yang, the cycle of life expanding, contracting.

Love thyself, for these gifts of life, for each person, each plant, insect, animal, and every living thing beat to the same rhythm of life blooming, changing, evolving, with infinity vibrating in all that is.

Personal Purpose

W̲e are all directed by personal purposes we create. In our drive to feel valued and authentic, we are motivated by dreams and passionate desires. So we refresh our goals and seek avenues to bring these goals to fruition. This is the natural progression of life, where our personal purposes can sway with the wind and continually redirect our courses. People create, and this is in the heart of living our purpose.

Are we failures if we do not follow through with our goals?
Purpose has its purpose. We are a collage of purposes. Purpose enlivens our desires to move forward, discover new horizons, explore the adventures of life. It gives us courage to create. We change professions, change direction with our plans, as they morph into new goals and expressions of our feelings.

Purpose evolves and is designed to do so in our life journey. People create miracles every day, fulfilling ever-changing purposes. Magical, passionate feelings are the driving force of purpose, with each step in our creations being equally vital and important contributions to all of life. Regardless of how meandering our route through life is, the ever blossoming crescendo of love is our destiny. Purpose has its purpose. And so it is.

Virtue

W e are made of attributes, with the full potential to mature these attributes into virtues, such as fortitude, temperance, kindness, patience, forgiveness—to mention a few. This energy of virtues has all of our ingredients in the energetic composite of who we are. Virtues are born of perfect love. In their fullest capacity, virtues hold our totality of being. Our abilities to grow and change, to become better, lie within. Awakening more fully to our guideline of personal excellence of virtues, our attributes gradually ascend into their fullness.

As you read the following words holding the descriptions of our virtues unfolding within, you will realize the steps of wholeness of self rising up to greet you. Each personal recognition of an inner truth allows a new interwoven fabric of love to grow, a strand of goodness to open within and enhance the flow of energy, an energy of God's love announcing to you the potential of growth into your personal perfection.

Our virtues hold our basic core makeup of love being ignited within each morsel of our new recognitions of life. These travels of self-discovery have taken us on smooth and bumpy roads to self-recognition, but we all want to feel our inner confidence building, savor our defined purpose blooming, and taste our oneness with all of life.

Our virtues have always been within, and now our virtues are expanding into the perfect ingredient of our radiant selves rising to a new level of reborn energies, lifting our beings as a new day dawns within our self-discovery process.

Part 2:

Take Charge! Recover Your Wholeness of Self

Take Charge!

It's up to each of us to take responsibility for our personal growth. We can start with truth—truth that goes to the art of inner vision and understanding of an inner truth. Pointed at the heart of life is a story that seems complex but holds three simple viewpoints from one's higher perspective.

1. Never hold a grudge.

2. Never place responsibility on another for our choices.

3. Hold light on all things for the clarity of a final truth of goodness to be recognized.

How do I use these points now to create better outcomes? I feel like a victim to circumstances beyond my control. Why am I so confused when making decisions?

So you waffle in self-esteem, looking to others for approval of your actions? Does another control your affairs in order to feel needed? What can you do to change these off-balance feelings?

The Creator gave the Ten Commandments to give guidelines for self-improvement to people. They became laws in a way, and fear was introduced into their translation.

But, rightly so, they are good guidelines to life and show that good judgment can bring a good result. Bad judgment brings a less-than-desirable result. Our thoughts and feelings certainly influence our choices, with many resulting in these less desirable outcomes.

Why do we feel we cannot change our feelings, change our content of thought?

Maybe we can allow the leader in each of us to take charge of our own life and no one else's. This is a starting point.

Could it be that empowerment is scary or unknown? Or could it be denial of our true identity of self?

Either can be the underlying factor that causes us to make choices to disempower ourselves, because we feel we cannot stand up to our truth.

Do we even know how?

This is a personal journey of self-discovery, but it is said that "the riches of the soul prevail in tenderness of spirit and a kind heart expressing."

Why not take a moment to look inside and take an inventory of those hidden feelings? If you need to write down what you discover, then do. This action shines the light of clarity upon the subject. And don't forget to ask your soul and your divinity to assist you.

When we look at the thinking patterns of people, mostly they show reactive states of acting and manifesting experiences. However, our Creator, our God Source walks side by side with the true self and sees and feels life in a more clear, decisive way.

Consciously partnering with God Source, like asking for help as in prayer or sitting in receptivity as in meditation, allows the result of this thinking to bloom into a more radiant, self-expressive result. Allow yourself to know that as you have grown in your understanding, you have come to an apex point that brings the energies of the new and the old and the in between to a cumulative sorting point.

This may be feeling a bit chaotic; however, as these energies come to the apex point, it is a still moment, the moment when all energies agree to climb the ladder of resolving lower, unbalanced frequencies and bring them into a higher resolve of themselves.

This all feels as if it has no calmness nor systematic value, but in fact, it does behind the scenes. The antidote for now is to relax and release anxieties, discomforts, and concerns to your divine spirit, the part of you that partners with God.

As the arrow of balance delivers our concerns into the heart of healing within our divine essence, we can allow our issues to leave without concern. We open to the gifts of change. Many times resolution comes with recognizing our feelings are different.

Issues and imbalances do us a great service as stepping-stones into balance and greater understanding within. We give ourselves a precious gift of light shining its truth upon our disturbances, with a pure, undiluted result.

Now is the qualifying time of your abilities, the time to apply your new-found wisdom to bring forth the rewards of balance and harmony in your lives. Start applying what you have learned.

How? How do I partner with our Creator?

Be aware. Pay attention to your feelings. Can you feel a stirring within? It is time for an inner housecleaning, getting in the corners where the energies of trapped fear hide.

Take charge! You are the boss. Think about and clarify your truest wishes and desires. Do you have higher perspectives of yourself and your life?

Now take time to really focus on these desires and dreams, keeping them up front in your mind's eye at all times. It is these desires that manifest in a manner of ease, for you have primed yourself for this desire.

Simply recognize your thoughts are the dynamic that blooms within the fruits of life, for they contain the frequency of what the intent is. Who else but you is in charge of your life? Who else?

The mirror of life does not lie, and the proof of the ability to apply a new face of decision is upon us. Granted, all changes and recognitions of life are a process of understanding the dynamics of change. These principles have been expressed by many. What holds truth for you? It is your choice.

Reclaiming Fragments of Self

Our lives hold the unique ability to stabilize one's self with love. As we expand and grow on our inner journey through daily experiences and choices of action, we signal the body to internalize the qualities of the experiences and harmonize its energies. We acquire a new vibration within our energetic body and create a memory of each event.

Whether we feel good or bad about our experiences and choices, our minds evaluate our lives, depositing memories like files on a computer. So now we are filled with excess baggage of energies resonating of the past. We have stored them, neatly tucked away as reference materials. These fragments of energy are established now with labels and compartments in our beings, that hold our light in little pieces in these files of thought and memory.

This is how we function and live our lives, day to day, with many of our feelings based on the focus on the stored memory energies.

A reckoning point of self comes in these times of rapid change, a reckoning point of cleansing and reorganizing our accumulation of the old versus the new. This inner transformation of change often creates confusion, and people struggle with these changes. Along with our efforts of inner change, earth changes are increasing. The cleansing process quickens, and chaos reigns in our world, reflecting the chaos of our inner beings.

What's happening and why? How am I supposed to handle this inner chaos with all of the craziness around me?

Now relax. It is not a doom-and-gloom scenario of no recovery into wholeness of being, but hopefully a case of willingness of spirit to unite in harmony with these current changes happening, not only inside of us, but in all parts of our lives.

Collecting fragments of the past means, initially, being aware that parts of us have been given to the experience and are alive in the deposit of energy as memory. These locked-away energies leave us with a reduced capacity within for the new, refreshing, vital energies of change showering our beings now. Once we release the stored energies and increase our energy capacity to receive and use these new, vital energies, then the new energies can usher in a wholeness of one's spirit at a rapid recovery rate.

How do we reclaim these stored light deposits of self, feelings pushed away?

Well, the number one focus can be acknowledging the energy and focus given to the past and, secondly, simply embracing our ability to be flexible with change, an ability that is becoming alive and well in all things.

Let the hand of life open and flow within. If there is no space inside for the new, refreshing moments of growth, we create great discomfort inside, and anxiety and stress may be felt.

Why?
Because life is all about change, and each person's destiny holds growth and change.

Can one control this event?
No. It is impossible, for to try to stay stagnant in life will not be. As we negate the old and the fragments of the past are extinguished, we release space and energy to embrace life in the now. Your light energy returns to convert itself into the new references for life. This feels like a new lease on life.

With this new space open within, you can easily move into the light of change. Dance in harmony and joy as you participate in the conversion of the old into the new, a changing of the guard, a fresh day dawning into the warmth of harmony in all things. This is the natural act of evolution with a cumulative effect and is the hierarchy of life expressing, as the new richness of the moment contributes to the all and life moves on.

Our journeys through life precede all else with the unique ability to provide the opportunities to embrace each moment fully and each new inspiration with open arms. Here are a few stepping-stones for your journey.

1. It is important for you to create alone time for yourself. Choose a regular time slot for yourself. Maybe put this on your calendar.

2. Find a space for your inward process where you won't be interrupted. Inward quiet times create openness for receptivity, insights, guidance.

3. Pick events that you truly choose to participate in.

4. Allow yourself to make your own decisions from your own sweet spot, your own desires for what you choose to be experiencing in the here and now.

5. Accept and live life fully present and current in the now.

6. Honor your truth and inner knowing. Feel this. Make it real.

7. Acknowledge the nudging inside that comes forward to guide your sharing, a gentle push that is always with us.

Now, as you reclaim your precious light, and with the expansion of your new conscious understanding, the richness of life literally blooms each moment into a fuller radiance.

Honor Thyself

Ｗe have heard our bodies are our temples, to honor them, take care of them as the holy vessels that they are, but have we really understood how important our bodies are?

Why are our bodies called "temples"?
Through the ages our physical bodies have assisted us to move, feel, and digest life. Our bodies are God's creations that give us our holy, divine instruments of being. The human body was designed to work together as one unit with our soul and spirit, a body-soul-spirit team.

Disjointed in expression, we have lost this insight through our distractions of life. Most likely we focus on our complaints: *I hurt. I have this problem. I don't like how I look. I would be happy if I were different.*

Granted, we have illness, misalignments of our energies manifesting in our bodies as disease, unrest, problems. But if we could pause and realize that if we had no physical bodies, how could we enjoy life? Any part of life as we know it, problems and all?

Have you ever talked with your body as you would with a friend, voicing your complaints and asking your body to help you understand how to make changes to help it feel better? How about appreciation, gratitude, or love for this precious vehicle for the mind, soul, and spirit to express through? This is what is called "body talk."

Try this body talk! It is amazing how changes can occur in all parts of the body, when we actively include the physical body in our daily focus of life.

When we focus on improving our bodies, we often just think of beauty. Beauty is skin-deep, and we are fixated on our image of beauty. We diet, exercise, take pills, have surgeries to create new physical images, but what happens on the inside? Image is just that: an image that becomes illusive, changes, ages, declines.

How can we address our inner beauty? How does this work, and what motivates our physical bodies?

We want to feel better, so we try to change how we look and so on, but we can also turn to the basics of the inner workings of our bodies to address our inner beauty. Try listening and witnessing your breath. Your heartbeat. Become your body's best friend.

Body wants to be included in the process of life and not ignored. Body is like a child who has temper tantrums when excluded. Its stored anger and disappointments can pull us out of alignment, expressing in the body as disease.

If acknowledged, as we learn to work intimately with our bodies, bodies assist with healing. Remember that focus creates. A mentality of "poor me" creates and is reinforced, and, with more anger and other negative emotions, it can solidify into illness.

Body often responds like a child but holds eternal wisdom as well, saying, "I am as eternal as the soul and spirit. Without me, there is no progression in physical life." This recognizes the eternal nature of the body-soul-divine team, that they are in this together. And that's as good as it gets!

Try visiting with your body. Listen and be sensitive to your body's responses, your inspirations that bring light upon your body's requests. For example, "Body, please help me release this. I know you feel my discomfort. I am ready to release the anger, disappointment, sorrow," and so on. State the underlying emotion, feeling into it, breathe, and by degrees, release the layers. You will be well rewarded for your efforts!

If you already practice the art of appreciation of oneself, congratulations, for you are the victor and the caregiver of the temple and vessel of God's creation, your precious body. You are honoring your body. The next time you get that massage, say thanks to your body and enjoy it!

Fortitude

ⵣ

Fortitude fuels our inner journey of growth with continuous changes. Throughout history, fortitude was described as determination and a strong will. A broader meaning allows the flexibility of using one's will in a strong way but holding the light of courage in the mix.

Courage of spirit is an example of the strong, energetic vibration that this word, *fortitude*, holds. Fortitude, above all else, takes us on a journey of determination to fulfill one's desires.

How can I develop this fortitude of being?
In our self-discovery process, there is a gap between our reality and our desires. The following practice can be helpful to bridge the gap within us between the heart and mind.

1. With inner vision, draw an energy line from the mind into the heart, and from the heart into the mind.

2. Invite your desires, maybe one at a time, to ignite and light up the lines, going back and forth between the mind and heart.

3. Fortify the line of energy with your passionate intensity of focus.

4.   Notice whether communication between feelings and thoughts
     smooths and noticeably improves. Acknowledge outcomes.

This gap bridges itself when our desires ignite, providing the passion to
dig deeper, allow more, and persevere to rise above our perceived limitations in our internal and external realities.

The push to excel is natural and is motivated by our energy of fortitude.
And we will find the crossing into smooth sailing along our inner journey of awakening, for a beacon of radiance pierces reality with intention,
not to be met in failure.

Why then do we apply fortitude of spirit in such a diluted way, mostly
failing to boost our inner strength, failing to be consistent?

In our choice of this inner journey to heal into wholeness, we experience the elevated frequencies and cleansing of oneness of spirit. As you
dredge up the residue energies of your experiences in your life, you will
revisit and re-experience the associated feelings that come up with these
experiences. It would be devoid of the necessary steps for you if you were
to bypass the feelings of the experiences that have helped you grow, and
change, and become more of who you really are.

It is necessary to witness within the violation of your truth, the violations
of your inner beings, and the violations of your soul as well. Your spirit
is steady and holds the isness of your divinity, and it is the overriding
director of who you are.

The invasions that have denounced you, as individuals and as a collec-
tive of the human race, are betrayals of energy that fulfill their necessary
needs in bringing forth realizations to make a choice of validating their

presence as your reality or negating their presence as your reality. These energies have provided a service for growth challenges to us.

The choices are ours to make in continuing the denouncing experiences or claiming our inner strength. This is a choice of inner strength that comes up for the use of inner commitment, the use of inner knowing, the use of standing tall in who you are, without the invasive energies that bombard you, trying to take a little piece of you to fortify their existence.

Fragments of light are fragments of ourselves that have been given away from reactionary behavior. Reactionary behavior is a weakness that allows the vampires of energy to feed upon this weakness. These vampires may be individuals in our lives that lean on us and deplete our energy mercilessly, in their supposed weakness or ignorance.

It is an experience that brings inner strength forward to claim its total purpose of why it is in charge of your totality. These deeper strengths are known and are very well in place deep within humanity. It is the outer layers of personality—of weaknesses of inner knowing expressed in a diluted, separated, segregated reality you live in—where the splinteredness of the full impact of the energy is not felt. While environment can oppress us, we can claim our inner strength and call it forward to change our behaviors and support balance in our lives.

We make a fine attempt in applying the pureness of the fullest description of this energy of fortitude. Many touch on their inner goodness in responding to the needs of others in a time of disaster, accident, or trauma.

Our deepest desires of goodness can rise to the top of our list of inner virtues. When a person realizes their inner character of being, they can call on this power to sustain them when needed. We all aspire to the heroes of life and appreciate the hearts of people who rise to the occasion and demonstrate the awesome powers stored within our recesses of purity in action.

How can I strengthen my fortitude and be more conscious of this result?
For now, as many struggle to understand the simple things of life, it seems like a faraway possibility to bring our potential of attributes forward. We each have it in our soul plan to do so. Invite fortitude forward with the clear intention to persevere in your goals of life, whether these are healing into more balance, more love in your life, better health, or more resources to achieve these. We can also intentionally direct our arrow of truth (picture this) to pierce the confusion to land in the clarity of truth in our choices. And if help is needed along the way, Creator is always side by side with us, ready to lighten our load, until we can productively use every opportunity of growth.

It is soothing to just know we will eventually achieve our goals of life. It is soothing to believe that this will be, all in the loving order of our creation of life. Recognize your potential. God blessed humanity with many pristine qualities that will come into fullness in your timing. As we achieve our destiny of wholeness, all of our God-given attributes, having matured into virtues, are available to take full rein of our total abilities and apply them in our lives.

Just think of acceptance of this. Mull this acceptance over in your mind. This simple process will create movement in your changes. That is all that is needed. Rest at ease, for all will be shown to you in a blessed state of recognition that God has your back! And so it is.

Temperance

Temperance is seen as a body balance within that brings one into a moderate balance of heart and soul, with a calming feeling like an even keel, or a temperate climate, gentle and nonthreatening in its makeup. Peace, joy, and love all live in a state of temperance.

How does this temperance begin, and how do I keep it going?
Well, now we begin the story of self-love. This part is up to you, for all people have different feelings. Our story of recovery is a gentle one, for we have expressed the need of looking within to create our maximum abilities of growth and understanding of life and where we are in the mix.

With this in mind, listen for the little voice within that reminds us of a peaceful nature available in us at all times, accessible and willing to become a reality, instead of choosing drama as our initial response to life's challenges.

Sometimes anger or other residual emotions take over, and we just lash out, wanting relief but creating more damage in our actions. We all have felt judged, rejected, denied, and violated, either by ourselves or others.

How do we gain temperance when we are polluted with old emotional baggage?

In the release and cleansing of our inner baggage, it is necessary to witness and acknowledge our stored pain. Our challenges of painful feelings give us a choice of inviting our inner strength forward, to call forth our fortitude and claim our inner knowing, to stand tall in who we are. This brings us into temperance of spirit, a balance that serves us well.

These teaching lessons have been necessary to enrich the soul and could not be replaced with serenity until the purpose of their existence in our lives has been validated. Our painful experiences have served their purposes to bring inner strength forward. They have done their service for us and can be released in a tremendous step of self-recognition, as we bow to the heart of truth.

As we awaken to ourselves as masters of light, or even have an inkling of this possibility, that realization turns on the light bulb of self-discovery. We can begin to discover the energy lines of pureness of love that lead into our blooming process of expansion of being. Feel this bubbling effervescence of life where the cool spring waters run.

This energy is the hiding place of temperance of spirit. Invite this refreshing temperance into your life. Let the cool spring water of calmness soothe your being. You can choose and intend a better balance inside, leaning into temperance instead of drama. Let this be a self-soothing process.

When we practice bringing balance in thought and action in our lives, we leave behind the need to create extremes in behavior. When we recognize our pattern of creating drama, and then work to reverse this pattern, our reactionary behavior in life can turn to the opposite direction of the calm, still waters of self.

Well, where is the excitement in life, if I am always calm?
The radical shifts of the ups and downs of feelings settle into a smooth availability of joy, pleasure felt at a new level, and compassion blooming into an all-encompassing feeling of pure ecstasy.

All of us walk the tight rope of creating balance in our lives. The ideal goal is a temperate spirit that is filled with the richness of love, a feeling that harbors the maximum joy of life. Who can resist the communion of love in this manner?

We, as humans, were created to vibrate in harmony with the richness of our inner being felt and appreciated for its content. As we develop our temperate spirit, we can excel in life. As we climb the ladder of self-acceptance, the blessings and tidings of great joy with fulfillment expand. Our almighty, universal heart beats with one masterful destiny, and that is returning to our exquisite master plan of being.

What better way to live life? As our arms open wide to embrace the gifts of life, we begin to know that we are one with all that is, and what a blessing of love that is!

Caught within Disease and Sickness

D aunted by sickness leading to chronic health situations, the people of today have an epidemic of sorts. The rising illnesses are marching out of control.

Why would the average person, the wealthy person, and the people with mounting hardships feel so powerless to heal?

Within our focus and translations of our feelings lies the illusion of disempowerment. Turning our focus inward shines a light upon our limited perceptions. As we acknowledge our confused and negative thoughts, our feelings of self-empowerment can begin. Our intention to change our feelings and attitudes can let light shine in, and the healing begins.

How can people with illnesses recover as they struggle with their various problems?

Many people, including children, are plagued with imbalances of their physical and mental bodies. There is no one answer for the cures of one's health, but there is a hope of recovery as the blessed individual climbs into themselves and looks into the diseased parts and evaluates the feelings they deeply and sincerely feel.

Cracking the shell of darkness within begins the release of the stranglehold of past pains, fears, and entanglements and brings a fresh breath of hope, a lighter load to carry on our path of self-discovery.

What about innocent children?
Children's innocence of spirit reminisces in its wholeness, but misalignments of the body and soul, as soul's purpose of recovery marches forward, sometimes plays out in early childhood. Life's process marches forward, but with little regard for those who are small and new and fresh born to life.

These manifestations seem cruel and unkind, but the will and determination of love blesses all beings as it intervenes in love's behalf, anointing the innocent with a holy blessing of recovery, in varying degrees, to the physical body, the soul, and spirit as well. Each experience is a blessing and an instructive step back to wholeness, whether or not we accept or understand this in our sorrow of loss. The process of life does not hold a judgment. It acquires its agenda from the needs of the individual to gain from the experience in more wholeness and radiance within the individual's holy plan of life.

Growth is achieved through life experiences. The rewards of all experiences are the return to wholeness of spirit and the enriched love of being. This holds the eternal qualities of the blessing of life.

Solace to Heal the Broken Heart

There are no words to soothe a grief-stricken heart. As time goes by, a softening of the heart can relieve the pain but can never reverse the loss, whether it is the loss of a loved one, a dear friend, or an animal, or whether one is simply grieving the loss of connecting with one's own self.

In our intricate web of emotions lies a deep-seated sadness as doubts, fears, loss, pain, and suffering fester in our feeling nature. We were given the pureness of heart to feel love and its temporary losses deeply and exquisitely.

Sometimes we do not recover fully from these experiences, and those of you who are struggling with recovery from your wounded and broken hearts, are addressed with reverence and admiration of an endearing soul. As one seeks peace of mind, maybe escaping the pain in the softening heart, tenderness of spirit enlightens and is enriched.

Eventually the process of reawakening to solace of being blooms and begins to infiltrate our being with a stillness, a quiet place of refuge, a soft end and new beginning of the timeless movement of change.

Solace received is solace cherished. It is a state of remittance of peace, tidings of hope. It is an inner knowing of the fullness of one's abilities to rise to the occasion as the victor to purpose and acknowledgment of who we are and our abilities to embrace this process. Incrementally we move closer to believing we can do this.

When solace finally comes, it is a space of acceptance and understanding rising from the depths of our soul. Solace is the result of our faith, hope, and trust in the process of life and the inkling of wisdom prevailing. The state of solace is eternal, with far-reaching ties to the still, small voice of patience, virtue, and authority of pure bliss that creates the state of mind that can mend the broken heart.

It is through the heart breaking and healing, repeatedly bruising and healing into a greater, more expansive love, that we reclaim the richness of our wholeness. This greater love finally expands into a glorious radiance that embraces all as loved and cherished, as perfect and pristine in the heart of the beholder, at one with all.

This then is the gift of the broken heart, the ultimate healing that has taken eons to achieve. Humanity is now on the brink of this experience, many courageously embracing their pain with a dawning hope of emerging into the richer wealth of lovingness. This emerging hope is welling up from humanity's stillness, finally triggered by the maturing readiness that finds its release in the pregnant pause of the bruised and healing heart.

"Seek and ye shall find. Knock and the door is opened. Ask and it is given."[v] For all of you in the pain of loss, of disappointment, of whys, pause in stillness and allow. As your hearts heal, a greater love emerges, blessing you forevermore.

And it is foretold this mightiness of spirit resides in all people, and they are the victors of the precious gifts bestowed upon them. And so it is.

Time

In this moment of time, the straightforward meeting of love infiltrates deeply within as an essential element of who we are. As we intentionally embrace change, we accomplish another goal as we climb the ladder of self-acceptance in a richer, fuller way.

Time is elusive, for linear time is in the physical realities, but eternal time dictates the whole of life within and without. It is immediate and it is in the future; however, now the past lies in dormancy, as it falls away, never to be reborn again.

The immediate advantage is the dramatic eclipse of change, a foreshadowing that has come into readiness. The fruits of life are ripe and succulent to greatly prosper in the dramatic shifts in consciousness within humanity, exploding into action and rising to the occasion.

Time, dear ones, holds the magic of change and is the cornerstone of events within a given space of all eternity. Slow down the clock, and the magic of the moment becomes all there is. Speed up the clock, and you fast-forward through life without notice of the magical events bursting forth in the moment.

As the mind adapts to a new way of thinking, the breathtaking climax of life unfolds, and the birth of the new reveals itself. Proclaim your eternal time clock, and witness this new expression of personal understanding. After all, you are the focal point of you, and the anointing of oneself in its full radiant glory shall come to pass and will be felt and witnessed.

You see, life is love expressing at every moment. Catch a glimpse of its beauty, and rest in the solace of heart, for a new day is dawning, and time reveals itself in a new way.

Your eternal time clock holds the truth of your existence, but surely know this moment reveals the miracles of change into the goodness of your being, becoming fuller, richer, in its existence and relationship with all that is.

Embrace your eternal time clock, and liquefy the stoic existence of restriction and crowding of linear time. Let it unfold within. Invite it. The guidelines of linear time are necessary to exist in the three-dimensional reality, but to awaken to the unprecedented flow of life is another step in expressing, feeling, and embracing personal freedom. All is well. All is well.

Final Days

Once upon a time, people scattered to the winds, finding new ways of meeting their needs, and remembering their longing to unite together in the universe, and to know their existence was important.

Now in the final days of preparation for the unknown, it seems imperative to pay attention to the prompting of the inner heart calling your name. It is important to pay attention to the final preparation of transition of being into a completely new form of being, a being that opens to clarity of purpose within the human race and addresses personal steps of improvement needed to accomplish the latent goals of yearning for truth in all things.

Arise, dear ones. Embrace your changes for the better. Deny the archaic pull of the past, and use your God-given talents of discovery to allow new visions to prosper.

In the next part, "Enlighten Your Soul," a new curve, a fresh aspect, of truth will awaken new potential in one's thinking and expansion of self. Stretch and enjoy the enlivening expansion of being, foretold throughout history, that is happening now.

And now, this personal expansion is in the eternal time frame of events. As linear time collides with eternal time, the unison of life bursts forward to allow a new expression of the whole of life, cascading into current moment reality. And so it is.

Part 3:

Enlighten Your Soul

Isn't the Soul Already Enlightened?

Pleasantly surprised, we face the new and fresh idea that our soul has an evolutionary program and is expanding and growing in richness.

The soul was given to each conscious human being as the navigator of life, purposely identified with the master blueprint of each person to evolve in personal abilities to experience changes throughout the walks of life. The soul expresses the framework of life from the blueprint in the qualities of perfection, as given from its Source of creation.

But is the soul complete? Does it know every step of the way?
No, for all parts of life including the soul, expand, grow, and enrich themselves with a brighter essence of what it is. Life has the ultimate purpose of expanding and becoming grander than the current expression of itself.

Forevermore, we apply these guidelines of life to our everyday activities. We, of course, have the ultimate example of our perfected selves in the examples of goodness of expression that grow in compassion and now become a universal activity that fortifies the all.

All of life is blended with a common strand of life. That ignition of radiance, as our compassion grows within, is our propeller of direction and service to ourselves and others.

Most likely the way of growth is a simple event of love in action. Most likely, all movement within life as we know it is motivated through the expression of love, as layers upon layers of expression of love unveil themselves with the constant movement and expression of life.

What purpose does the soul have?

The soul is the navigator of one's road map through the living of life, with the experiences felt along the way propelling us to take action, to change. The energy content of these experiences holds the qualities manifested into action through each person.

If the motive of thinking produces qualities of hate and evildoing, then the acquiring of the pure radiance of love does not enter the equation. But, if one bumps their head many times and wants changes to take over to improve life, then the door opens for the expression of love to grow and prosper.

The soul holds the potential of one's ability to progress in life, expressing to the degree it can grow and change. The enlightenment of the soul is the advancement of its content and potential of each individual in a grander scale of what it is.

We don't think or sometimes even understand these principles of life, but really it doesn't matter, for the focus of life in the moment with the richness it holds affects all parts of us.

The texture of the soul is you. The content of the soul is part of you. The activities of life expressed through the soul is you. So why not get to know you a little better? Shake hands with your soul, and begin a new partnership with yourself. Enjoy the journey.

The Kiss of Compassion

Compassion is the energy that comes from the heart seed of love, the purest form of love expressed in your world today. The feeling of compassion blesses the heart with a warm, exquisite richness penetrating the body with its royal frequency of love, not to be confused with the tugging of an emotional attachment of reaction. This stage of feeling vibrates at a lower frequency of attraction.

Compassion is a love that extends warmth, concern, empathy, and caring to another, where kindness and benevolence take over as compassion embraces the recipient in tenderness.

So why don't we feel the depths and wonder of this love ignited now? Why doesn't the world unite in compassionate living and being?

The story of love is ever moving and changing in all things. In the eye of the storm rest centeredness and calmness. We can be still there with Creator in the eye of the storm as life swirls around us. As the halo of love descends around us, we can expand in our abilities to feel true compassion for life and in life. This is the energetic space of the birth of compassion.

How does compassion affect the soul?

Transparency favors the truth of a subject. Transparency of our feelings with our selves creates a special blooming within the soul, and the soul expands its energy in a more refined quality of itself. This form of love is the highest ingredient in loving unconditionally. Fortunately, as we continue through our intentional journey of growth, many have begun to sense that this expansion of self is right around the corner.

How can this be?

In this time, in this space of the world and all of its activities, the act of sorting and cleansing is upon us, bringing the pus of old, stale, unloving energies to the surface to be washed away in God's hands, as divine providence is within the changes happening now rapidly, succinctly, and with a higher purpose.

The acts of nature, the challenges, and changing within all, take us on the journey to recovering our wholeness and stability as a human race. These immediate changes register within the soul, and life begins to change, because of the changing of the guard in motive and divine evolution of self moving forward into a more complete expression of itself.

All people now can rise up and claim these gifts of love. We can unite our efforts to truly become free and lift our beings into the eternal freedom of change to become our wholeness of being.

Thus the soul recovers itself and holds the new potentials of growth for each individual to prosper. This is a team effort, body and soul, as we rise to the common thread of physical life expressing fully in change and recovery of the pristine beauty held within the bosom of our souls.

As we lighten our frequencies within, meaning the quality of the content of feelings and emotions, of beliefs and patterns of life, we lighten our souls, we lighten our spirits, and together we heighten our abilities to receive the kiss of compassion unto our beings.

Lift and lighten. Lift and lighten the consistency of all things. As we enlighten the body, we enlighten the soul and spark our spirits to dwell in oneness with all—our body-soul-spirit in oneness with all. And so it is.

Will the Real You Step Forward?

Feelings are the foremost ingredients of the soul. Our eyes are the windows of the soul radiating our love and light. If we are in overwhelming fear or pain, our eyes reveal our distress.

The deeper, purer the feelings, the higher the frequency of love within. The feelings based in compassion rise to the top of the class, as they fill the soul with its enriched program of love.

As our feelings become richer and more refined in content, we recognize the difference between emotional, reactionary responses and feelings led by compassionate responses.

"It is easier for a camel to go through the eye of a needle, than for a rich man to enter into the kingdom of God."[vi] This parable gives a guideline to reveal the despair and hope of many who try so hard to unite with their heaven on earth.

It is not with riches, surgeries, substances that we achieve our lasting goals of happiness and compassion. Some of these actions can hinder our progress. The struggles of life seem fraught with anchored limitations, with doubt flitting around each endeavor. If doubt takes over, the cycle of change for the better seems even more elusive.

So how does the real you step forward?
Herein lies the real work!

I don't see how to do this! My health is failing, and I don't want to talk to my body. That is stupid! I don't want to change. I just want a simple answer of how to heal. I am who I am, and I'm too old to change and do this!

Individuals feeling this are not alone in their pain. Many of us have old stored anger, fear, pain, illness that seem persistent and stubborn. Our negative thoughts and emotions are creating and contributing to our misalignments and disease.

How can we change our experiences with these? We seem to repeat these indentured patterns endlessly, a deep rut of repeating history, like there is no way out.

As the stored emotions that fuel these archaic patterns build upon themselves, increasing in intensity and illness, we are desperate to escape their hold on us. Stuck in negativity, needing acceptance, understanding, validation of our worth, we wonder why others don't appreciate us and value our contributions. And anger grows until we are ready to explode.

We look to others for reflections of acceptance and validation of ourselves in our quest for self-acceptance and self-love. We need these reflections for acceptance with all of our unpolished attributes, the hidden gems that hold our highest potentials, until we can come to our own self-acceptance and self-validation.

In the mounting pain of tangled negative emotions, we may reach our limits and surrender, finally willing to do what is needed to escape our indentured emotional slavery. Here is where we can choose to partner, instead of going it alone. We can seek professional help. We can ask the Divine, our Higher Power, God for help. A lighter load and a way to get better—a doorway to peace, understanding, relief, health.

With clear intentions to release archaic emotional patterns, even in the midst of the anger and pain, we can persist, knowing that as we gradually let go of these emotions, it leads to a blessed life of peace and love. We begin to trust our plan!

The process is gradual, ongoing, progressive. Give it time. Hold your intentions. Do the work. Believe in yourself, that you have a plan to come home to the heart of God.

With your inner spring cleaning, your inner healing continues, and the residual stored emotions actually melt and convert into a deep-felt, compassionate response, releasing their hold to be replaced with a refreshed, new, authentic part of you expressing. Ultimately, it is up to each of us. As we embrace personal changes proactively, the world around us magnifies itself in texture and beauty.

Now is a good time to pause and play in the simple pleasure of life, for the fun of life is not just for the senses of children to enjoy. With your new perception, all of life is fresh and new.

What's the difference between emotions and feelings anyway?
Emotions seems like knee-jerk responses or even survival responses. If feelings are beyond survival, how do I mature into more feelings and fewer emotions, less reaction?

As we all ascend in self-observation, living life with all of its filters, senses, and interpretations interacting and creating our emotional responses, feelings rise as the emotion or attachment to an event translates with a meaning of it.

This cycle grows in depth and service to humanity. The process of seeing through an emotion is the development of creating a feeling to the degree it was felt. As we grow in authenticity, our emotions are gradually released with their stored light into our real feelings, converting the stored energies into available light capacity to participate in present-moment reality. Granted, this cycle of creating responses has its layers and textures.

Let's get back to the basics of feelings versus emotions. Step forward in willingness to feel deeply without restraint. Observe your feelings, letting them be what they are without editing content. This helps to bridge the mind of interpretation into the heart of knowing. Not knowledge, but intimately knowing the qualities of life in a fuller, more prosperous way.

As we acknowledge the difference between feelings and emotions, and examine the richer qualities of life, we begin to know our I am presence. This ultimate, highest level of love, called the I am presence, is where the body-soul-spirit team is active and has reclaimed the ability to love deeply and fully, our destiny of love reclaimed. Feelings felt at this deep level of love are very different from the intellect collecting knowledge and its attachment through reactive emotions.

The I am presence is accessible in the asking."I am," spoken as a decree, calls forth our wholeness. Step forward to feel deeply, without restraint, as you focus on your I am presence. Be willing to feel the intense pureness of love in feelings versus the less loving feelings held in emotions.

Our soul is the advanced version of our physical body with all of its senses, emotions, and feelings. When the person advances in awakening, the soul awakens into a more advanced quality within itself and lifts the bar of potential from within.

The master blueprint of our lives is the active ingredient in and throughout all things, and by degrees, this life map influences our advancement in the growth of the soul. After all, what is the purpose of life if not to grow and change, uplift and expand, within its very core levels of God's creation of us, with the ultimate calling of living life with all circuits working fully? Priceless? Yes! Totally fulfilling? Yes! What could be better? And it always will be, for it is a never-ending story.

Does the Soul Listen?

Our souls easily listen, hear, and change to the beat of the eternal drummer of life expanding, regardless of our current states. And the sound reverberates within. "I am listening, and I hear you," the soul responds.

Are we listening? Maybe that is the question.
Listening, hearing is an art of perception. The finesse of life lies within hearing and feeling the sounds and meanings of simply pure communication between the world and our perception of it.

We know that our perception and translation of life is how we hear, see, touch, and feel our lives through the aids given us for our smooth, vigilant, and prophetic courses of action taken in our lives.

How can we listen with the art of perception, becoming fine-tuned and vigilant in the smallest, most detailed way?
Most of us react to life in conversations, conversing on any subject, and we depart from hearing the incoming delivery, as we are conjuring in our minds the answers we feel are what we want to respond with.

Where does the original intent of delivery go?
Before the words of the message were truly completed, they were altered in quality within the listener because of the need to respond in reaction instead of fully listening to the message given.

All dialogue between people holds special messages, if we are sensitive enough to hear them. If not, somewhat like fast food that satisfies the immediate need, the richness and fullness of the flavor is missed as the communication is fast-forwarded into completion.

What happened to relaxing into life, savoring life, instead of rushing by in a hurry to go into the next event of life? Are we shortchanging ourselves?
Pushing past life in an abbreviated perception to the details of beauty and solace all around is an empty arrival of self, just getting by, like skimming through life, rushing into the next event.

The art of really listening to the motive of life's gifts is lost in the hubbub of everyday demands. Our busy life becomes a determined activity that misses the arrow of love that could pierce the unfolding chaotic events. Our spirit, our common thread of life, is ignored with the illusion of life rushing by.

Our soul, the very fabric of our physical existence, is impacted through all of our sensory perceptions of life, and records in energy all feelings, thoughts, impulses, and frequency exchanges. If we don't enrich our soul with the complex flavors of our experiences, it can't enrich us.

Remember, life runs on eternal universal time, not linear time. It is possible to simply open to a motivation of love, slowing down, remembering the Source of who we are, taking a moment to listen, hear, and feel the minute details of each word. Every moment can be a vacation for the body, mind, and soul. Savor this richness, for it holds the sacred core of expression of love in each facet of itself.

Listen, hear, feel, and see what your life really means to you. And so it is.

Authenticity

"How great thou art! Oh, Lord, My God, when I in awesome wonder..."[vii] Wise beyond reproach, our identity arises into its full potential.

What does this mean?

A wise owl sat on the branch of a tree looking over the widespread face of the landscape. He blinked and, with awesome wonder, praised his existence just by sitting there observing the landscape. He blinked again. "How wise I am! How wise I am!" his very essence proclaimed. This wise old owl has gained his reputation as a symbol of cunning thoughtfulness, proud and sturdy.

What has become of the wise old owl within us? Where is the feeling of certainty in who we are, with confidence and assuredness? How can I be authentic?

Humanity is an exquisite creation. We are human beings. This is the most authentic creation there is. My dearest ones, in all your glory, you stand in perfect authenticity of who you are. Just simply recognize this. Claim your perfect self, authentic throughout the fiber of your existence.

We, in the living world, are not feeling or living from our perfect state and potential, but we have it. We strive every day to understand ourselves when aspiring to our lofty thoughts through our dreams, desires, our creative endeavors.

The point is that, as we grow and change for the better, we follow the master calling of our own creation. We may be temporarily blind, asleep at the wheel, but now is a special time to awaken from the long, deep sleep to our conscious ability to recognize our attributes, our potentials, our purpose, and live our very existence more fully.

Granted, our reality is specifically designed to have the disconnect experience of opposite polarities that bring comparisons forward. But the dark night of the soul sees its perfect light as the light of life shines dearly within.

Our soul is reminded of its authentic self from love showered upon it through the awakening experiences of life, bringing more and more opportunities to claim, live, and enjoy the exquisite you. Talk about a road map to wholeness! We are!

The long sleep of humanity has now passed, and the sparks of light shine brightly, as the soul is refreshed in and of itself with chords of harmony, light upon the authentic creation it is, and the reclaiming of its perfect blueprint of existence.

We all aspire to the inner calling of our knowing that we are greater than we sometimes feel. We are greater than we realize, and we are authentic in our witnessing, in awesome wonder of our very existence. "How great thou art!"

Kindness

Kindness is the master feeling of love extending to another. The feeling of kindness holds a tenderness beyond reproach and tells the universe how love changes the very fiber of life. When kindness is felt, the heart swells to hold a special radiance that is very naturally shared with the world.

To be motivated with a kind deed says, "I care. I care for you. I care in a deep, special way, and I want to help," as my love springs forth from my heartstrings, extending in a most loving way.

The soul knows within its being that kindness is the ingredient of its radiance that is the inner lining of its existence. Witness the simple feeling of kindness within a child.

A little boy crossed a bridge over a stream. On the other side, he paused, listening to the water splashing, crossing over the rocks, bubbling, rushing. He sat down on the bank, and a small bug crawled over his leg. Thoughtlessly he swatted it away, sending it flying. Then another bug crawled over his leg. This time, feeling a magic in nature, he watched this little bug closely, seeing the details of its small, wiggly body.

Time to move on. He got to his feet and wiped the dust from his pants, strolling down the path. The magic followed him. He was feeling happy! "What a good day this is!" He began to skip and even hum a little. "What a good day!"

Warm and comfortable, he thought of his grandma. She had a garden. He didn't like her garden, because every time he visited, she asked him to help her with it. But today, to his surprise and even pleased with himself, he wanted to stop by.

As he approached her little cottage in the country, he smelled something good, and his mouth began to water. Eager and hopeful for a cookie, he thought about helping his grandma this time as he went to her door.

"Hi, Grandma!

She smiled.

"I have come to help you in your garden! Do I smell cookies? May I have one?" Cookie in hand, he went straight to the garden with a glad heart. He was happy and thought, "This is a good day!"

Helping another person nourishes the heart with a long-lasting, nurturing effect. Each moment felt in kindness swells into the very core level energy of love and ripples out into the universe. Yes, the universe!

All energy is shared. All thoughts are a shared event. So as you can see, we as a people are very important in the scheme of life.

How does kindness enlighten the soul?

Kindness ripples through the soul in a wonderful pattern of light fulfilling its purpose. Each soul disregards relationships that do not embellish its existence. So to live without a soul holding the perfect blueprint of our ever-changing experiences and growth would go against all of the soul's creative programming, and the physical existence would be incomplete in and of itself.

Kindness embellishes the soul, and the soul embellishes the physical. As kindness ignites, our feelings of compassion form a symbiotic relationship of harmony enlivening, exposing, uniting, and encouraging our ever-moving life. And the soul prevails in its holy purpose in life.

Patience

Patience, patience, patience is a virtue, hard to practice, but only pretends to be hard to do.

How can I become more patient? How can I soften my inner turmoil when my brain is busy, very busy at times, conjuring thoughts, ideas, planning, incessantly running its programs?

Throughout our years this precious attribute, patience, has been promoted many times and used as a role model in developing our personal characters and the fiber of our beings. Let us look at a deeper meaning of patience. The energy of patience is a blend of the stillness within and the active mind. It combines these energetic values and brings forth the opportunity of creating a state of balance within.

When we focus on quieting the mind, we at times become combative in our own thoughts and seem to argue with ourselves to find a quiet space within to feel the refreshing peace of mind. Many techniques are given for meditation and prayer practices for quieting the mind.

Where does this fit in developing the virtue of patience?
It is part of the equation of developing leadership in oneself. However, the main ingredient in acquiring more patience of spirit is to simply go directly to your spirit, as if addressing a dear friend you wish to visit with.

Your spirit is your wellspring of goodness, stillness, creativity blended in harmony with the divine aspect of you.

How do I contact my spirit?

Sit quietly and simply ask to feel your spirit presence. As the mind still runs its programs, you can observe yourself in a new way. Introduce in your thinking process the desire to feel calm, peaceful, centered in your stillness. Pause and be in your stillness. Feel into it.

Patience is expanded upon energetically within, as we take the seat of observance of ourselves and do not get caught up in trying to control the mind or even our spirit. The virtue of patience revolves within the balance of our very being, with our opposite energies within us coming into a neutral feeling.

How does this help me?

In our quest for more understanding of life and ourselves, we flounder at times in this process. But as we become aware of the intricate parts of ourselves, we can then evaluate the bigger picture of our personal growth.

Patience creates the flow of infinite love directly into action. It brings light upon life with a nonjudgmental eye and lifts our spirit into a compassionate state that overrides the lower, denser vibrations holding less love within their consistency.

To rise to the occasion to enjoy and share patience is a wondrous event. As we allow a tolerant state of mind to expand, we provide a great service to ourselves in our inner quest of discovery of who we are, and of course, to others in our lives.

Patience is truly a virtue, the stepping-stone into a more tolerant and loving you.

Forgiveness

"Forgive them, Father, for they know not what they do." [viii] This quote, given by the Christ in His time of peril on the cross, demonstrates the dramatic fullness of compassion felt and given to the world.

To this day the effect of the intensity of forgiveness reigns as an eternal truth of love, reflecting to all of humanity. The act of forgiveness is one of the most powerful steps in changing negative feelings into positive feelings.

How can I forgive another when I don't feel it, but think I should? And how can I forgive myself for my failure in releasing judgments and blaming others?

Holding another accountable for their actions that trigger our feelings, like resentment and anger, are anchors within that keep us in a lower vibration of our beings. These feelings anchor themselves deep within the heart and soul of our being. They hold up a red light.

In the process of attempting to forgive, we sometimes create another layer of personal guilt, feeling guilty over the need and stress of trying to let go of blame, anger, sorrow, and caught in the midst of this process. "Shoulds" do not fulfill a real energy movement of healing within. More guilt added to the failure of performing the shoulds of life only clogs channels of perception more.

And guilt just piles up in the recesses of our minds and hearts as additional pieces of inner baggage to carry around. No wonder we feel weighted down and struggle to get a handle on change.

Our desire to grow and change is a conscious decision to do so. As many have searched in their hearts for guidance and assistance with their understanding of oneself, it has been a search that brings fruit to the seeker. Forgiveness—to fully forgive another—means to change our need of attachment to feelings that are crammed into a special box of self-righteousness, of being right with opinions and judgments of people and experiences. The more we sustain the feeling of being right and another being wrong, the saga of determination to hold fast to these feelings continues to be a stoic stop sign to changes for the better.

As we let ourselves feel these feelings with the intent to release them, they begin to soften and become more benevolent. If we choose to explore another's opposing viewpoint or reasoning with a growing understanding and acceptance of the person's process, then one such opening in our heart and thoughts can create a feeling of personal freedom rising within, with a big sigh of relief that swells and feeds the soul. A touch of compassion releases us from our personal entrapment.

As compassion is allowed to grow within, the intensity of the grudge, anger, resentment begins to soften and change, and slowly the walls of negativity disappear, leaving a new, clear space to feel this stepping-stone to achieve a better you. As compassion rises within, you can feel the act of forgiveness has completed its cycle.

Here are a few stepping-stones to assist.

1. Observe fully, with an earnest request to yourself, the anger, resentment, personal grudges, and the need to be right, remorse, the need to retaliate—whatever emotions and feelings that are ready to reveal themselves.

2. Allow yourself to feel each stored emotion. This means don't edit the process. Dive directly into the pain, the fear, the need to be right in the situation, whatever rises to the surface. Be with your feelings.

3. Allow the flow of a change of feelings around the subject to spring forward to replace the old with a new love vibration that you hold within always.

4. Believe in yourself, with a growing ability to have faith in your personal process of renewal of self.

5. Let this changing of the guard within, these energy shifts, marvel you with your release of the stranglehold on your own self. Celebrate each increment of change. Give yourself a smile.

6. Embrace a sense of relief, and then the new degrees of compassion that rise up.

7. Be conscious. Be still. Be allowing. Be free!

Our inner housecleaning requires a clearing of the corners of oneself, allowing the cobwebs of the past to be swept away, not to return.

Forgiveness! What a powerful word of change, for deep inside, we are truly accepting and forgiving our own being for our judgments, opinions, the literal and stoic interpretations of right and wrong, and the personal gratification felt from the false prophet held within, and sometimes acted upon in aggression toward another.

The act of recognizing the power in focusing forgiveness on oneself creates the active benefit of feeling joy and awakening into your joyous spirit, your true self. And all is well.

The Soul Rejoices

The very texture, value, and composition of our unique makeup as human beings arrive at various levels of consciousness and understanding of ourselves through our many experiences of life. Granted, we have different levels of awareness, different calibers of being. As we grow into more loving individuals, we register our changes of awareness in consistency of feelings and astute ways of changing every part of who we are into new impulses imparted unto the soul and received by it.

These energies, with enhanced calibers of frequency, imprint new, enlightened energies into the soul, and the soul rejoices with this tribute to the advancement into one pure radiance held between the physical existence and the unique existence of a higher level of purpose held within the soul. As this union of the physical and soul fulfills itself, the individual climbs the ladder into harmony with all of life.

Could we call this process of the physical body and our soul partnering our destiny, individually and within the human race?
Yes, most assuredly, and with dignity. Perhaps we can accept and fulfill our prophecy of oneness with God and all there is. After all, we are the twinkle in God's eye. We have an inheritance of returning, claiming, and prospering in full development as a thriving race within the scheme of life.

"Twinkle, twinkle, little star. How I wonder what you are."[ix] Look into the mirror, my loves. Your light of existence is my light of existence. I am that I am, and we are one. And the soul rejoices!

Still Waters of the Soul

As you ponder, gazing into the horizon, envision the ocean. How does it appear? Is it choppy, with the winds creating whitecaps and currents creating large swells moving to and fro?

Or is it pristinely calm, mirroring the sky in its reflections?

Sit and ponder, feeling the possibility of seeing the ocean calm and in harmony within, as a movement from left to right, right to left, to and fro.

Observe, feel, and witness the balance of your being, the inner creation of stillness within, the still waters with harmonious currents moving back and forth, back and forth, to and fro, to and fro, still waters soothing the soul.

Part 4:

Embrace Oneness of Spirit

Rock of Ages

"Rock of Ages, cleft for me. Let me hide myself in Thee."[x] Our spirit is our rock, our foundation of who we are.

What is spirit? How can I connect with my spirit? Spirit seems elusive and intangible. How does this make sense?

Our total selves in our creation of being holds three major categories of our makeup: body, soul, and spirit. Each is special and serves a definite purpose, acting through the God-given attributes of human potential.

Even so, mostly we feel disconnected from our unity in all parts of us. This is the journey we all travel to reunite together in our self and bring harmony to rest in our laurels of love. It is quite the excursion to follow our lead into the precipice of growth, many times jumping into the unknown, only to find a new perception of life.

As we add many avenues of expression in our growth, we become a living collage of energies mixing, matching, uniting, expelling, and changing our lives to bring us into a greater part of ourselves.

Well, why then would we not feel our spirit as the collaborator of life? As children of God?

Rightly so, because we have the very core level matrix of our divine Creator within, and our spirit is our divine aspect of self. What better way is there to feel connected to all there is? What better way to feel God's love in action when we are related and part of one another?

Just because we don't clearly feel this at times, does not mean it is not true. As we awaken from a deep sleep of our existence, we experience many aha moments that show how we can coexist and prosper with all parts of ourselves and others, who mirror parts of us.

The creational rock of our being is not a new addition to our makeup. It has always been present, from our very inception, always will be, and holds everlasting life within. Solid, dependable, everlasting, and fulfilling love eternal is who we are in the bedrock of our existence. What a great relief to feel the truth of this very stable part of who we are. We have roots set deeply in our planet Earth, for we are one with her as well, with connection in spirit deeply rooted in the whole scheme of things.

Stand tall, children. Stand tall. You are the rock, the stability of life, the flow in all things, and you are everlasting. To doubt is futile.

Why?

It goes nowhere. Doubt holds no real stability in lasting energies. It dissipates into the ethers, as truth is discovered, as we steadily climb our ladder of life's discoveries. We may feel like we failed, but again, this is not a real truth, for failure holds no lasting power, and again is released into the ethers and takes its rightful position in the back of the line.

Stead-worthiness of spirit enfolds us within the womb of creation, for in our inception, we became part of all that is.

You are a rock.

You are at one with your divine Creator.

You hold the torch of truth within.

Open and awaken to who you really are.

Most unequivocally, you are the child of God. "Rock of ages, cleft for me. Let me hide myself in Thee." And so it is.

What Does My Spirit Have in Store for Me?

Spirit, body, and soul remain in energetic ties to one another fully, but in our physical life, we do not pay much attention to our abilities to connect fully, consciously, and clearly with all of us.

I see a big gap in communication with my spirit. How do I connect fully with my spirit? This will take some fixing!

The joy of all is to recognize you have the ability to fix this gap. "Listen to the still voice within"—we have been told this as a guideline in communication with our spirit.

Through our genuine intention to seek solace within, we rest with our mind directed to our spirit and its abilities to alleviate our anguish. Expressing to our inner knowing, our spirit sends through the energetic connection and therapeutic waves of loving frequencies, constantly transmitting back and forth within us to our souls, to our physical minds and feeling natures.

Just because we do not consciously feel these transmissions does not mean they are not happening. Now tap in.

Tap in? How?

Most of our recognitions come from our thinking processes. Some of these recognitions are feelings of great depth that the conscious self is aware of. But as we witness the expression "know thyself," we look for the answers to do so.

First and foremost, to awaken to your synchronistic values of the body-soul-spirit connection takes a determined intention to do so. And here are a few guidelines to awaken to your spirit.

1. To practice connecting with spirit, and creating your conscious body-soul-spirit connection, start by choosing a spot of refuge that allows a quiet atmosphere where you will not be interrupted.

2. Advance past your doubting mind to simply feel the space beyond the busyness of the mind. Detach from the chatter. Be still. Be quiet. Feel. You can look at yourself as a small child who is guided into a focused exercise. Guiding our focus takes a little practice, but the rewards are many if we pursue our desires.

3. Be consistent with your practice, and let go of any temptation to wonder off in thought. If your focus can experience a little second of stillness, you can feel where you meet yourself, your spirit.

4. As you go forward with regularity in your practice, you will feel different. Monitor these feelings. Take time to

acknowledge this has happened. This builds your sensitivity within you.

My dear ones, this is your next step, and it will take you to the sweet spot of feeling your spirit, visiting with yourself on a grander scale.

Is this obtainable?
Oh, yes! Many find their solace within the stillness of being, and many witness an expanded inner knowing that is spirit speaking to you.

How can I hear or feel this inner knowing? I'm not sure I can do this.
All people have the potential to become aware, in their exclusive ways, of connection to their total selves. The willingness to change actively is a necessity, for in this action taken are our personal breakthroughs into the world of hope, magic of manifestation, the partnering with all parts of ourselves building into a fine-tuned instrument of harmony, love, and everlasting laughter and joy.

Be your witness to inner change. Stand tall and unite with all parts of who you are.

Focus creates and focus enlivens. Become astute in your observation abilities of all things. Visit with your spirit as old friends do.

Listen…listen. You will hear.

"I dwelleth in the house of the Lord, My Lord, My God of my being. And this is good." And so it is.

Feeling My Way to the Top

O ur intellect stays in a dominant circle of reason. It was not designed to replace our feelings, only translate life from our quality of thoughts. In order to go into ourselves with a Get Out of Jail Free card, we must travel the path of our inner knowing, which is motivated by our feelings.

This is a wonderful pathway to explore on our inner journey, as the magic of the unknown is driven forward to witness and experience.

The universal heart beats to the same drummer your heart does. And the universal heart will respond with the greatest of love when asked to do so.

You see, it is all in the asking. My dear hearts, remember to simply ask for your road map of life in an adventure of discovery. As we travel this pathway of love, we anoint ourselves with the key to unlock the doors of self-recovery. We activate the recesses of inner truth and begin to vibrate at a different level of our being.

This is the key to our success in granting ourselves permission to continue our marvelous inner travels of knowing. We travel inward in feelings and discover the richness they can hold. Why would we choose differently?

Now we are through the inner door of self-discovery and follow our promptings to look deeper and wider, to witness the expansion of our very core being. This expansion is very noticeable and feels at one with a new radiance and an inner glow.

Our world will never be witnessed with the same eyes again. And our flower of life begins to bloom in all its glory, a story unknown by many, but a story that is ageless in content; a story blessed with the integrity of our own creation; a story of a love affair with our own heart. What could be better?

As we rise in our consciousness, we activate new energy levels within and begin to elevate our very being. Holy waters run deep within us, and we kneel to drink the nectar of the truth of who we are. What a marvelous journey to travel this walk of life! Blessed are we to travel our path into our wholeness of being, for all people have a radiant destiny to follow. What is yours?

"Let there be Light, and there was Light. God saw that the Light was good."[xi]

The Spoken Word

In our physical existence, we were given the art of communication between one another. The challenge has been to determine what language are we speaking. Bilingual methods and translators of the spoken word have somewhat bridged the gap in communication skills.

How do we get ourselves fully understood?
We have been given the art of interpretation. This method leaves a lot to be desired, for the meanings of words vary and are understood in different ways.

It is said, "God ordained The Word and it was good." [xi] *So why the Word? How does this relate to my spirit and my soul growth?*
"The Word" is an application to apply the use of quality within each formed word in thought and in deed. The quality of thought formed within each word is the solidness of its foundation and holds the frequencies of the intention creating in the different strata of existence, with the physical world being the densest layer.

There are many levels of meanings, with frequencies that broadcast the different meanings. The same word, sentence, conversation can hold many levels of translation.

As the word is spoken from the mouth of babes, its innocence and purity seek its fit in energy patterns that are held within our soul and spirit. The frequency of the word with its intention deposits itself into the physical strata of energetic values. And our thoughts and words create!

This explanation of the inner workings of the Word shows the importance of paying attention to our creations from our quality of thoughts that are formed into the Word.

So our words create?

Yes, our power as human beings is to witness the creation of our words and thoughts. Don't ever think that innocent ramblings or idle conversation do not impact the world. As we see with new eyes, as we understand with new thoughts and feelings, we can witness the manifestation of our reality, the manifestation of our physical condition, and the manifestation of life itself.

The Word was given as a free choice experience to determine our ability to choose wisely what we say, to honor our power to manifest in our reality, and to rise to the occasion of participating as cocreators of every living thing, and to know, above all else, we hold the torch of manifestation.

We hold the torch to higher learning, conquering all things that do not serve our highest good. As we reclaim our destiny of love, living this reality within us consistently, this love creates. As we open to living in a responsible manner, where we know we are creating the outcomes around us, with the understanding of our abilities, with a glimpse of our potential as a human being evolving, we then can feel how important our choices are.

Important to whom? Is it important to evolve into a better person? Is it important to feel appreciated for our demeanor, our kindness, our interaction with others in a loving way?

Yes, for not to become aware keeps the darkness of the soul intact, and the quality of life spirals in a downward movement into the dungeons of a self-created hell. We have choice. Why not use it well?

As we advance within, the need for words diminishes, as our thoughts become strong, pliable, and thought-provoking, for our communication skills expand to a more refined way of communicating our true thoughts without confusion. How refreshing!

There is a graduation taking place, graduating beyond belief into a new reality of clearly understanding the purity of thought, the undiluted ability to clearly focus and transmit ideas. With refinement of ourselves come many new and exciting abilities that change and refine our natural abilities and God-given attributes.

Will I have this refinement in my lifetime?
Possibly, for our ongoing potential in advancement of consciousness is a progressive event. As we speak in a state of alignment with the body-soul-spirit team speaking, with one pure voice for an ease of manifestation, the innocent, clear intentions quickly excel and advance within.

These experiences of growth keep on moving, growing, expanding, as we step up the ladder of life's expanding qualities of itself. And so it is.

Innocence

The baby cries as she opens her eyes to the world for the first time. As her voice announces her presence, her innocence is felt by all, embracing her arrival in the world. And her adventure begins. With a feeling of protecting this innocence from any harm, all hearts are naturally prompted to assist and provide sustenance, to enjoy her radiance as she adapts to the world.

Each of us possesses this innocence of spirit. Pliable, moving, strong, and vulnerable, the energy of innocence begins at our inception and seems to wither as we engage in life. Simplicity and all it holds would be close to the energy of innocence, but this precious value within us seems to vanish into the deep recesses of our being, as we move through our life challenges. Maybe a tear rushes forward, as the sadness of this loss floods one when witnessing the qualities of innocence in others.

Our innocence is our ability to be vulnerable to the teachings of life, to be open to the freshness of life as it plays out in and around us. This breath of fresh air clears away the debris of doubt and fear. It removes the residue of caution that inhibits our ability to refresh ourselves.

How can I reclaim my innocence in my life now?
Well, it takes a desire to find the sweet spot within that surrenders to life's innocence and lays down the guards and walls built up, brick by brick, to fortify one's astringent mind and heart.

Mighty is the self that can be in a humble state of mind. As one collapses into the ability to become humble, flexible in thought, and willing to let go of fortified walls and concrete structures of belief systems, a soft texture, a strand, a sweet calling to the innocence of the child within, can rise again.

And now the world can be a benevolent teacher, and life is viewed through the eyes of the child. You! And always held in the swaddling clothes, rocked in the arms of God.

Be of good cheer, for your values of being are always present. Open the gift of innocence that awaits you to bask in the sunlight of your spirit. And enjoy your inner journey with its growth process of fulfilling God's promise. And so it is.

Gratitude

G ratitude's word energy has a lasting service to mankind. It brings light into the dark recesses of the mind. Gratitude reminds us of a small portion of ourselves growing into a larger part of who we are.

The attitude of gratitude expresses well. We can form a bond with this sacred energy from within, allowing the inner flow of gratitude to rush forward, as a river fills a dam and a dam fortifies a nation.

We are becoming servants of gratitude in feeling, for each moment realizes its perfect image of what it is, and this perfect image is recognized with the eyes, ears, and feelings of the beholder. Gratitude shared comes back to the grateful tenfold! What an honor to serve our own self in honoring our process of growth!

How can I fill my heart with gratitude?
As we seek, the response is given. When we address the quality of the asking, the receiving is automatic. As you can see, gratitude, another attribute of inner qualities of self, rises to the surface. Our purpose now arises in the quality of the asking with reverence, for focus expands; focus accumulates and integrates with its every fiber of what it is. Ask and it is given.

"Fill me, oh Lord, with thou bounty and bless the restoration of my Soul."

Prompted in vigilance of spirit, we accumulate the advancement of our spirit, the advancement of our soul, and blessed is the physical self with a new reverence of life.

Gratitude begets gratitude, and it grows and expands within the breast and sanctifies our existence with a special blessing in its wake. Granted are thee, in this process of accepting your faith, trust, and goodness of heart magnifying throughout the world. To remember our gift of becoming greater each moment is our gift to all people, to all animals, to all plants, and every component of life and becomes the new awakening for each and every one.

Embrace gratitude, and the holy veil of light descends upon you. The holy essence of light descends around you. The fragrance of flowers encompasses you, and the perfume of all enlightens you.

Blessed be this day of transformation within the hearts of men. And so it is.

The Blessing of Grace

The state of grace is a state of completed love expressing in and through us with all of our being invested in the acceptance of this gift. When we recognize this energy of love, it is all encompassing and allows an enhanced state of existence to unfold within. Our energetic body vibrates in an elevated state and denies all else, as its persuasive love inherits itself with unity for all.

How can I feel this state of grace?

The energy of the state of grace is a fullness of spirit that enfolds one in love, as you ask for this love to become visible, tangible, and alive within. The silky smoothness of life in grace begins to occur through your desire to fully unite your physical body, soul, and divinity within, and then bask in the light received in this asking. Grace then comes about in degrees of sweet and eloquent outcomes.

Grace serves, for the state of grace is the glue that holds us close within, the fabric of life everlasting. "Amazing Grace! How sweet the sound!" [xii]

A Prayer of Grace

My sweet Lord, Father of all, we unite within your mantle of love. We unite together as we embrace the divinity of our being.

We unite together in your holy state of grace, for it fortifies our very soul and carries us through the rough, unstable times in our lives.

We give thanks and appreciation for this holy grace and blessings upon us.

Today, above all else, we ask to feel, unite, and collect all of our wits and abilities to focus our desire and intention to walk in the holy state of grace, within this world and forever.

We come, we come, and we receive this blessing unto our hearts.

My blessed child, you are My grace. You are My perfect creation that lives and breathes with a single heartbeat, a single goal to reunite with your fullness of spirit.

This is the purpose of your existence. Focus. Allow. Awaken. Each step takes faith in your travels home, home to yourself in a completed way.

Beauty

B eauty is in the eye of the beholder. Most innocently revealed in quality, beauty captivates all who find it in their interpretation of life.

Fragile, strong, delicate, and detailed, beauty brings to mind and heart a special appreciation of its lasting effects deposited within our very core being.

How does beauty change us? Does it affect spirit? Why does this special quality catch our attention with a special reverence for its very existence?

As rarely found as a precious gemstone, so lies true beauty in its purest state. Its rare ability to change a feeling, a viewpoint, an opinion, or simply an observation is quite remarkable.

How does beauty make a difference to me in my life?

Cherished, moved, loved and adorned, compassionate, reinforced faith, trust in creation, appreciation, melting into tears, motivated, adored, witnessed. I am sure you can add to this list of how beauty affects us at the deepest levels of our being.

We, as people, are transformed deeply and profoundly with the experience of beauty in all of its displays into our lives, whether a virtue well expressed, a miracle on display for all to acknowledge, or a marvel to embrace through the eyes of the beholder.

As our inner beauty intensifies, layers of our richness within grow beyond measure. Our senses begin to awaken, a gentle quickening to their enhanced abilities. We see life with new eyes. We hear the smallest sounds, and stillness becomes active within the beauty of its expression.

This radiance of beauty can take you away. Imagine: in the midst of nature, the crisp morning air fills your lungs with the fresh, pungent scent of pine, deeply enlivening your awareness. You gaze into the surrounding landscape, absorbing and appreciating its vastness.

Slowly you turn to a massive pine, awed at the expanse of her enormous trunk. Feeling her gentle pull, you wrap your arms around her, reaching only halfway around her girth. Sinking into stillness, you merge with her presence, mesmerized with the unexpected union. You seem to be one, as her exquisite nature fills your heart. Her overwhelming grandeur, her melodic resonance become part of you, and you flow into her, a compelling union never to be forgotten.

As your focus is directed inward, your body responds to the quality of the thought given. Positive, loving thoughts radiate beauty inward, and the body becomes more radiant as these are absorbed within. True inner beauty reflects these loving thoughts and becomes strong and vibrant.

In nature at her fullest, your mindscape is expanded. Soul is embellished. And spirit soars. In a God-given act of creation, the Master Artist imparts the exquisite beauty of creation, and we are moved with an intense appreciation and enlightening translation of the art.

The butterfly is a good example of nature's magnificent transformation patterns. She emerges from her cocoon a butterfly, with delicate yellow wings softly moving for the first time, gradually unfolding fully. She waits for the perfect moment to embark upon her new adventure, magically transformed, flying free into life as nature's exquisite gift of transformation.

Rarely seen is the exquisite beauty of nature in its fullest pristine state. We, too, are deep in the process of our unique, personal transformation. As we progress in our sensitivity to life, advancing in our conscious recognition of our fullness of self, we recognize the intense natural beauty all around us and within us, in every step of the way in our journey of fulfilling our master design of who we are.

Stepping into Perfection

Life is a series of stepping-stones providing small increments of change to be experienced in our journey into wholeness of being. Each step of the way is a leap into the joy of our potential fulfilling its unique purpose in the holy plan of life.

Each of us has a road map, a blueprint of our master plan of becoming united in a state of perfect harmony and bliss expressing through the radiance of the full potential of our creation.

What does that mean?
Your inner map leads to your destination of wholeness within and oneness with all, but your inner journey cannot be ignored. Participate with your transformation! Plan it! Use the stepping-stones given. Allow these changes and harvest the benefits of growth, for they lead to life in total harmony and bliss with all that is. Use your road map for an easy journey and arrive in love and so much more!

What is my full potential?
Great question! Energetically, we are a complex, intricate vessel of impulses, descriptions of actions translated from energetic impulses. In our fullness of self, we vibrate through new energy fields developed within.

These energies spark the pristine qualities of our full array of abilities to produce perfection in action.

For example, we have many intuitive abilities that express in our reality in a very diminished way. Our insights are not activated fully. Our desires are limited in quality, for we are not fully opened or expressing from the full ability for which we are designed.

Take a moment to scan yourself. Are you fully awakened to the intricate use of your abilities of instant manifestation of events? Inner knowing felt and expressed in its fullness? Vision that opens to inner vision capable of seeing and feeling the levels of life expressing in the universe?

Are you awake to communicating through the ability to transmit thoughts directly and succinctly to chosen destinations, whether a person or a group, both physically and spiritually, acting from your inner impulses of perfect alignment in body, soul, and spirit? Allowing love to fill your cup with its infinite unconditional abilities bringing a completed compassionate state of being?

Uniquely presented in fullness of self, you obtain the ability to become completely balanced in all levels of your being. This deletes all conflict within, all fear, all limitation of any kind, and brings one's focus into a pure, direct ability to see and feel completely in the purity of the focus.

As oneness of spirit becomes your reality fully, the dogmatic, splintered reality we live in fades away and does not influence us in the same way again.

How can this be? How does this happen?

Our abilities to become one vibrating being in complete harmony within, come from our action of taking each step of self-improvement, with the result and accumulation of change, working from new and capable energies integrating and expanding within.

Evolution, of course, is the motivator, but in this special time presented now is the unique blessing to accelerate our growth process. We have the potential, the opportunity, and the desire to do so.

Unbeknownst to much of humanity is the divine pattern of change marching forward, actively, swiftly, and most magically. We all march to our perfect drummer. We all have our process of self-discovery marching forward.

So how will this change my life?

It has been prophesied that someday we will live in a heaven on earth.

What does this mean? It seems I am so far away from my perfection. Am I capable of becoming whole now?

The miracle of life changing dramatically for all of us is made possible with the divine plan of salvation.

We have a divine plan of salvation? What does this mean?

Now, in this time and space, comes the deliberate act of prompting the divine calling of spirit to rise up and pay attention, for the destiny of humanity now accepts this calling. And it is said, "In a blink of an eye, we will awaken anew." [xiii]

How can this be?

Through our faith and trust that we are moving into our new way of being, we accept the very thought, the very promise of the actual experience of these changes now.

We prophesied the distant future for these miracles to occur. In all honesty, with the witnessing of cleansing chaos in all walks of life, impurities of a detrimental effect on health in our atmosphere, decay of self from expressing and living old, archaic patterns of thinking, brings major change to the boiling point for the planet and each and every one inhabiting the earth.

Any change, any vibration of energy affects the universe as well, as the rippling effect of energy with its qualities of what it is registers within all things. As you can see, this is a team effort, and we are major contributors to our welfare and the welfare of all.

But the divine plan, a literal salvation for the human race, is underway. Each of us will be assisted through the havoc of crises happening now. Whether the ravages of nature, the wounded hearts lashing out in pain, political unrest, or the earth's violent upheavals, we will be assisted through the desperate situations of our quality of living and surviving as the cleansing process of change increases. We will have the opportunities to reach out to others with helping hands, and receive the gifts of love that come as we rise to the occasion of needs around us and within us.

You see, the stale, sick, and demented energies now witness the intervention of light into the muck and mire demonstrating now. Light converts. Light heals. And light sustains all of life.

Breathe easy, my loves, for the truth of love is the victor. What is important is to bring focus and attention to yourself. Return to your center, the heart of stillness. And as in the eye of the storm, you may rest in the calm, sweet spot of peace, as you witness the blessed changes exploding all around.

Your virtues sustain you. Your desire to unite with yourself in a better way sustains you. The master plan of existence sustains you. It is not ultimately in the holy plan of life to have destruction and annihilation as the destiny of man. Life must fulfill the evolution of life, and that is life everlasting.

As the world experiences the upheavals of change, our challenges continue, but it is the very core faith of believing in yourself, living life as a human in full radiance as a true reality, that will sustain you in its truth. The wake of change in a dramatic way happens in the here and now.

Will I experience this in my life? Will I survive the disasters in nature, the choices of our government, the changes in every part of life as I know it?

We all have a soul plan that assists our experiences for advancing within, ultimately traveling home into oneness of spirit. We all have the potential to participate in these changes now or later. The divine plan of the return and restoration of each and every one is not determined by the limited expressions of life.

There is a master plan of a divine quality that enfolds all there is, and in a twinkling of an eye, all will renew. Heaven on earth is our reward, is our destiny, and will be our reality expressing.

Wouldn't it be nice to invest in the process of returning to a perfected state of being now? Each step taken leads us in a conscious way into a perfection of self to enjoy now. Standing in unison and love with the almighty force of change brings accomplishments and amazing returns, levels beyond levels of perfection in action, never to return, for you have achieved a transformation that does not reverse.

Embrace the rewards, for they are great. And we accept the lasting beauty of ourselves through and through. Destiny for humanity will prevail. And it is good.

In His Image

❧

"**S**omewhere over the rainbow…" xiv

Our finality of self is the accomplishment of raising our frequency into inner freedom. Simple yet complex, this process of growth delivers its rewards. Oh, yes, the rainbow's radiant perfection follows our self-development with the balance between all factors within us.

It was a divine promise given through the Creator's expression: "So God created man in His own image. In the image of God, He created him. Male and female, He created them…And it was very good." xv

Why then would our journey into completion deny us that very same privilege? Man was created in the likeness of God is the reflection into humanity, the perfect blueprint of humanity's potential of development. What an honored blessing this is! After all, who would deny one's own birthright?

Your search is an inward search that brings you to the resting place of home, the home within, as a child of God. The Holy Spirit is God's full reaching hand of truth, and when humanity gains its radiant presentation of self, His Holy Spirit shines and showers goodness upon the land, sea, and all there is. Heaven opens within, and the doors of self-discovery never close again.

"For thine is the kingdom and the power and the glory, forever and ever." And God smiles. And this is good.

About the Authors

Kathryn Rawlings lives in Arizona with her husband, dog, and two horses. Having received divine inspiration and guidance over the past forty years, she dedicates her life to sharing her wisdom with others. Rawlings considers it a special privilege to help others understand their fears, pains, and challenges so that they transcend those issues to unlock their full potential and recover their destiny of love. An author of five other books, she is gifted in turning complex principles into practical advice and helping people understand and embrace higher truths. She can be reached at purposerealized@gmail.com

Terry A. Spears, author of five other books, is a spiritual communicator, complementary health enthusiast, and a practicing pharmacist who has studied natural healing methods for 30 years. By sharing her higher perspective and profound knowledge of wholistic healing and divinity, she helps people enrich their souls and embrace their inner spirits. She loves rescue kitties, gardening, alternative healing arts, and cooking gourmet vegetarian food. Terry can be reached at purposerealized@gmail.com

Books by the Authors, available in soft cover book or Kindle.
Order from Amazon.com

- Inner Journey ~ Stepping-Stones into Our Destiny of Love

- Ascension Steps According to Isaiah, An Invitation

- Pasos Para La Ascension De acuerdo a Isaias, Una Invitacion
  (Spanish version of Ascension Steps According to Isaiah, An
  Invitation)

- Small Books Series:

  - Love Notes, Isaiah Snippets

  - Self Awareness, Meditative Practices

  - Wisdom of Change for Today's World, Verses of Truth

Endnotes:

[i] "Star Light, Star Bright." English nursery rhyme by Roud Fold, index number 16339, published late 19th century.

[ii]"In the beginning, God created Heaven and earth…And so God created man in His own image, in the image of God He created him; male and female He created them." Bible quote, KJV, Ge 1:1, 27.

[iii] "Looking for love in all the wrong places…" Song by Johnny Lee. Permission granted 9/22/2019.

[iv] The Lord's Prayer. A Christian prayer, taken from bible quotes, KJV, Mt. 6:9-13, Luke 11:2-4.

[v] "Seek and ye shall find. Knock and the door is opened. Ask and it is given."adapted from KJV, Mt. 7:7; Luke, 11:9.

[vi] It is easier for a camel to go through the eye of a needle than a rich man to enter the kingdom of God." KJV, Mark 10:25.

[vii] "How great thou art! Oh, Lord, My God, when I in awesome wonder…" Hymn lyrics, by Carl Boberg as poem, written 1885, published 1886.

[viii] "Forgive them, Father, for they know not what they do." bible quote, KJV, Lk, 23:34

[ix]"Twinkle, twinkle little star," by Jane Taylor, 1806. Published in Rhymes for the Nursery, by Jane Taylor. Public domain.

[x] Rock of Ages, cleft for me. Let me hide myself in Thee."From Christian hymn, Rock of Ages, by Rev. Augustus Toplady, in 1763.

[xi]"God ordained The Word and it was good." Bible verse adapted from KJV, John 1:1.

[xii]"Amazing Grace! How sweet the sound!" Lyrics from Christian hymn by John Newton,, English poet, published 1779.

[xiii] "In a blink of an eye, we will awaken anew." Adapted from bible quote, KJV, Cor. 15:52.

[xiv] "Somewhere over the rainbow…" by lyricist Ey Harburg, published 1939, arranged by composer Harold Arlen.

[xv] "So God created man in His own image. In the image of God, He created him. Male and female, He created them…And it was very good." Bible quote, KJV, Ge 1:27.

^{xvi} "For thine is the kingdom and the power and the glory, forever and ever." Bible quote, KJV, Mt. 6:13.

www.ingramcontent.com/pod-product-compliance
Lightning Source LLC
Chambersburg PA
CBHW060944040426

42445CB00011B/997